The Secret Life of The Eastern Screech Owl

Fan Song

Christian Fritschi

Edward Song

Max Song

TABLE OF CONTENTS

TABLE OF FIGURES

PHOTO GALLERY

ACKNOWLEDGEMENTS

Writing a book is a daunting task beyond just the work it takes to compile both pictures and information together. From the start, Christian Fritschi has encouraged me to share my journey with the screech owl family to a much broader audience. Christian collaborated on the content and has graciously translated this book into French, thereby expanding the reach of this experience. Many thanks to all the great effort from Christian Brysch that translates this book into German.

Motivation for this book also came from my two boys, Edward and Max. Their love and curiosity for nature pushed me to observe the family of screech owls despite all sorts of natural obstacles such as tics, poison ivy and mosquitoes. The boys' interest helped me overcome all the commuting time to the nesting site even notwithstanding of unwelcoming weather or fatigue. In the end, I'm grateful for the interest of those around me and hope others will find enjoyment of my stories surrounding the screech owl family. As any birder knows, observation taxes the patience of both the observer and his/her partner at home. My wife, Xiaolan, was extremely supportive and encouraging of my campaign to record the nesting habits and development of these amazing birds. Without a supportive family, I don't think I would have been able to witness these events.

I'm also really grateful to the owl family which provided me an intimate access to their lives and daily. I experienced many moments where I thought I could truly feel their love and passion for one another. To Danny, Jane, Anna, Alex, Christine, Charles and Sunny, you are the heart of my book and I sincerely thank you.

FAMILY TREE (2020-2022)

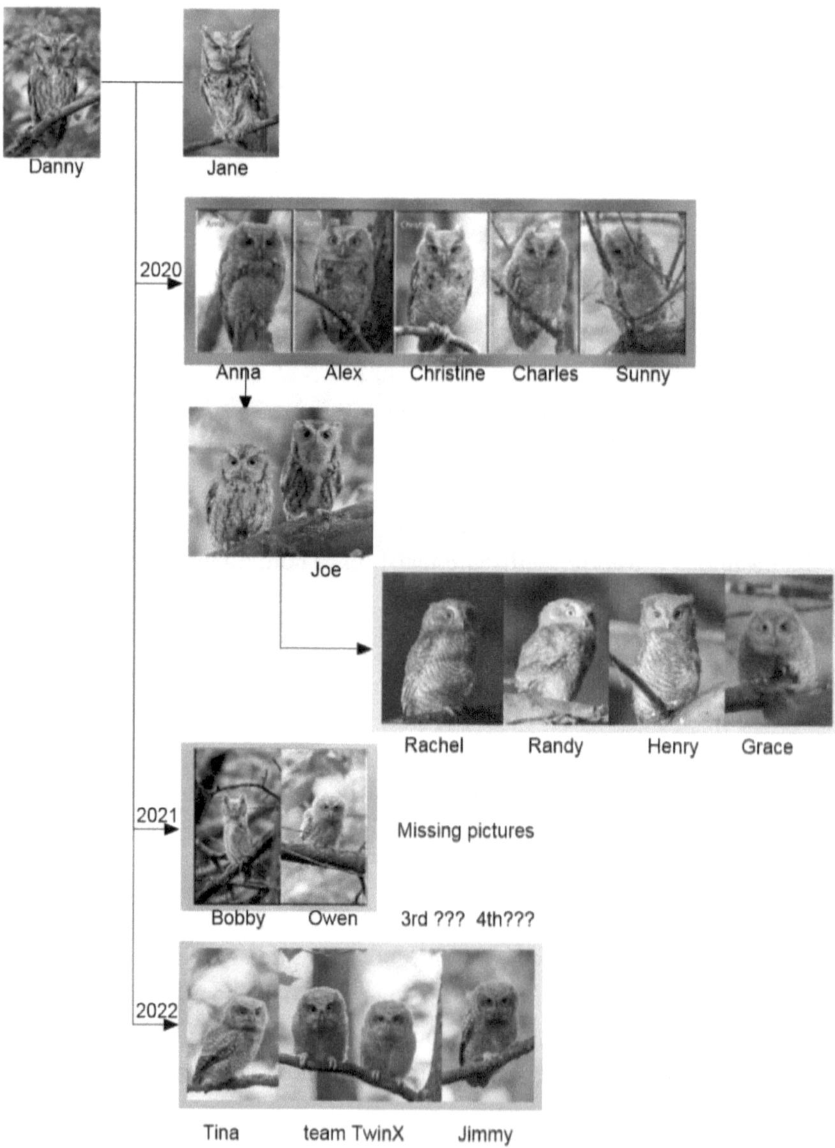

NOTATION & WRITING CONVENTIONS

[Fig #]: reference within the table of the figures.

[Note]: footnotes containing additional information.

[Ref #]: full reference citation located in the Reference section at the back of the book.

[Sec #]: section in the book.

[Tip #]: dedicated paragraph of my personal experience.

Tree stumps A, B, C, D, E, F, G, H and I: The favorite roosting locations of the eastern screech owls have been designated individual names.

> A: a great serving stump in 2020 but collapsed in May 2021
> B: Danny's sentry stump
> C: hermitage (winter palace)
> D: summer cottage
> E: Anna and Joe in winter of 2021 and 2022, outside the territory
> F: stump deep in the woods
> G: stump along the road where there is a small creek nearby
> H: stump under the nest of 2021 and 2022
> I: Joe's sentry stump #1, outside the territory
> J: Joe's sentry stump #2, outside the territory

Danny: the adult male screech owl.

Jane: the adult female screech owl.

Anna, Alex, Christine, Charles, Sunny: the five owlets of Danny and Jane in 2020.

Owen and Bobby: the two identified owlets of Danny and Jane in 2021.

Joe: the adult male red-morphed screech owl (in-law of Anna).

Randy, Rachel, Henry and Grace: the four owlets of Joe and Anna in 2022.

Tina, TwinX, and Jimmy: the four owlets of Danny and Jane in 2022.

mm/dd/year: date format.

INTRODUCTION

Owls are fascinating birds to watch and observe. They have many unique and endearing qualities: large heads with exceptionally large eyes, flat oval faces, iconic hooting calls, and a solemn demeanor [Fig 1]. My owl addiction began in 2008. Since then, I have spent thousands of hours observing and photographing them in their natural habitat. I have observed 20 owl species worldwide and encountered many owl families. These many owl experiences have created indelible memories and boundless joy; my life has been made richer by witnessing these amazing creatures and following their lives.

Figure 1 My addiction to owl watching

The eastern screech[1] owl [*Megascops asio*] is more elusive and difficult to spot compared to many other species of owls due to its small size, supreme camouflage, and strictly nocturnal habits. Once leaving the nest, screech owlets are particularly difficult to follow. Forming a close bond with this family of screech owls was extraordinary and fortuitous. I was able to follow the family through their breeding season between Feb and July 2020. This special relationship with the family allowed me to closely observe and follow their distinct life stages: courting and nesting from Feb to April, fledging and feeding of the five owlets between May and June, and owlet dispersal and gaining independence in July. It was truly a remarkable and memorable six months!

This book is a faithful record of my intimate experience with the owl family. Through my firsthand experience and many rarely seen, intimate pictures, I hope this book provides you front row seats into the secret life of the screech owls in ways never before seen.

Let the journey begin!

---

1 Unlike the "hoot" territorial calls produced by other owls, screech owls have their unique trill followed by rapid individual calls (although the sound does not resemble screeching or screaming) [Ref 16].

1 THE COUPLE

1.1 FROM 2015 TO 2019

In 2015, I had my first encounter with the screech owl Danny [Fig 2] in the Ottawa region (specific location not disclosed). Later in May of 2016, there was a report [Ref 11] about this same screech owl family with four owlets in the area. Unfortunately, at that time, I wasn't able to find the whole family.

Figure 2 Danny in the Spring, 2015

From 2017 to 2019, I was able to see this screech owl around Halloween time when all the fall leaves had fallen [Fig 3] [2].

Figure 3 Danny can be easily seen around Halloween Time, 2016

---

2 Throughout the book, 'Danny' refers to the male, and 'Jane' refers to the female adult screech owls.

1.2 THE SEARCH

Following a very mild winter, February 2020 brought reports of eastern screech owl sightings nearby [Ref 11]. The palm-sized eastern screen owl is a master of disguise. Its gray and brown feathers blend in seamlessly with the surrounding tree bark. Without detailed pictures of the area, locating them was a formidable challenge. I searched for days without any success and was about to give up until another owl report came in on March 11th. Danny, the male screech owl, had been roosting regularly in a dead tree stump[3] (i.e. Stump A) and the very news excited me. I began reading as many articles concerning screech owl behavior as I could and watching Danny whenever I could, believing Danny's behavior would guide me to find his partner.

Figure 4 Danny roosting in Stump A, 3/15/2020

---

3 The initial roosting site is referred throughout this book as "stump A"

Screech owls closely align their routine to sunset. In mid to late March, sunset is between 7:30-7:45 pm. On schedule, Danny would wake up 15 minutes before sunset in tree stump A. His daily schedule consisted of self-preening, yawning and wing stretching for about 20 minutes [Ref 1]. 5 to 10 minutes after sunset, he would hop from stump A to a small branch on a nearby pine tree [Fig 5].

Figure 5 Danny perching on a pine branch, 3/21/2020

Screech owls are highly ritualistic birds. After an entire day of roosting, the male always meets up with his partner by calling her with a continuous ascending tone, followed by a hurried trembling sound from its throat. This sound is very low and only people very close by can hear it [Fig 6].

The female emerges from her roosting place roughly at the same time. Upon hearing the call from her mate, they would chase each other for a while before settling down somewhere in the dark. I couldn't help but compare their courtship rituals with those of human romance.

Figure 6 Danny calling Jane, 4/5/2020

After watching Danny for 3 weeks, I caught my first glimpse of Danny's partner on 4th April [Fig 7]. Jane perched away from me on a small branch while Danny watched me from above. I hadn't named the owls at that time because I had no idea which bird was female and which was male. But I knew I had finally found the couple.

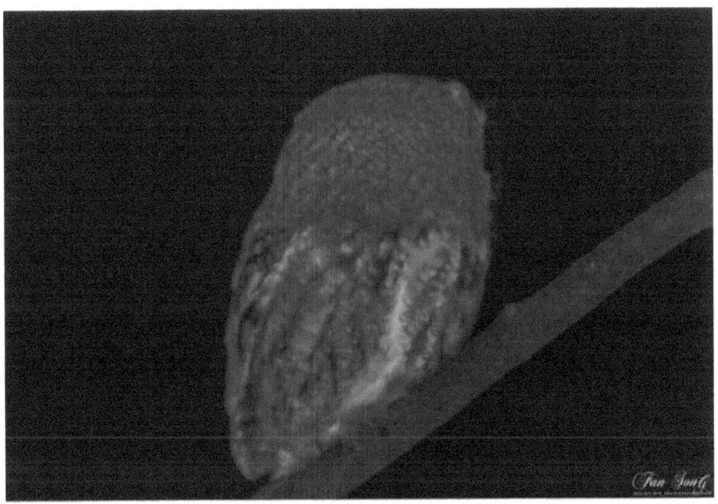

Figure 7 My first sighting of Jane, 4/2/2020

The strict and regular routine of screech owls helped a lot and after six days of visits, I was finally able to get a good picture of Jane [Fig 8]. I needed to find a way to differentiate the two owls. However, it was almost impossible to tell the difference in their appearance since they looked identical.

Figure 8 My first clear picture of Jane in the dark, 4/8/2020

1.3 WHOOO IS WHOOOO

Being able to differentiate between the two adult screech owls was a critical part of my research. However, I lacked crucial information and had very few pictures of the adult screech owls – especially Jane [Fig 9].

Figure 9 Jane perching on a branch, 4/14/2020

The gender of most owls can be determined based on size. This is not the case with the eastern screech owl species; generally, they show little size difference [Christian Ref 6]. Their small size, combined with the low light conditions, made identification even more difficult. For Danny and Jane, the facial disk, head, and collar stripes were nearly identical. The one subtle difference I found was in the chest stripes of the couple. Nevertheless, I still could not reliably differentiate them during the night-time.

As a last resort, I sifted through my photo archives since 2015 one by one in search of more distinguishing features. I was in luck! I found a reliable way to tell the difference – the dark mark in the cornea of Danny's right eye [Fig 10, 11]. This was a vital discovery because I finally had a way to tell them apart.

Figure 10 The black mark in Danny's left cornea, 2016

Figure 11 The black mark in Danny's cornea, 2018

1.4 COURTSHIP

Danny and Jane were definitely a couple because only screech owl couples share the same territory [Ref 4].

I often wondered what the couple would do when they settled down at night. Luckily, I managed to find them and discovered Danny preening Jane. For screech owls, preening is a form of courtship [Fig 12-14].

Figure 12 Danny preening Jane, 4/19/2020

Figure 13 Danny preening Jane (extracted from video), 4/19/2020

Figure 14 Danny preening Jane, 4/20/2020

2 THE NEST

After identifying the adult screech owls, the critical questions remained: Would they nest and if so, would they have owlets?

2.1 THE DECOY

I was becoming very familiar with the owls' routine; favorite perching places, hunting spots, and roosting spot: tree stump A. However, I felt there were more secrets to uncover.

Figure 15 A raven couple in the same wooded area, 4/3/2020

I was aware of two raven nests up in the same area and I would often see them vanish into the tall pine trees. [Fig 15] shows one raven couple. The female on the left waited for the male's (on the right) courtship. At the time, I was so focused on finding the screech owl couple that I missed the clue that the ravens were defending their territory against the owl couple [Fig 15]. I mistakenly ignored the places where the ravens were often hovering around or roosting. The distraction posed by the ravens hampered my search to discover the screech owls' nest.

One day, I suddenly noticed in a change in Danny's daily routine. This odd change in behavior caught my attention. He had been roosting in tree stump A since March 11th. It was as though he was acting as a decoy- to draw attention away from something else. Was this for attention, or was he hiding something [Fig 4, 6]?

My research told me that males protecting the nest will always perch in a location from which they have a clear view of the nest entrance. Male birds, during nesting season, will often try to divert attention away from the nest while the female is incubating.

I began to search for the nest site which had a good view of stump A. My search took a new turn as I started investigating all the possible cavities in nearby tree trunks. Unfortunately, I once again came up empty-handed.

There was a clue that I failed to take notice of: Danny's occasional glance upwards from his perch in stump A [Fig 16]. I often missed his quick glances but I finally realized that he just may be giving away the position of his nest through his glances.

Figure 16 Danny glancing somewhere above, 4/3/2020

2.2 THE MAJOR CLUE

Mid-April arrived. The snow was melting; spring had returned. Tree branches had begun to bud and crocuses were pushing their way up through the soil and remaining icy snow patches. Time was flying by with very little progress. I still had no clear idea where the nest was.

If Danny had given me the first clue which led me to the couple, he might just provide me with another which would lead me to the nest.

Figure 17 Danny roosting in stump B for the first time, 4/13/2020

April 13th was a very chilly day. As usual that day, I went to observe Danny roosting on stump A but he wasn't there. I was surprised he was breaking his routine. After a quick search, I found him at the tree stump B, a 3-meter-high dead pine tree which had been struck by lightning at some time in the past [Fig 17].

Danny's routine change caught me off guard. From March 11th to April 12th, Danny stayed at stump A for an entire month. Why did he suddenly relocate to stump B? My research paid off once again. The screech owl incubation period is approximately 27-34 days [Ref 4]. Could this mean the incubation period had finished and the baby owlets had hatched? With this in mind, I asked myself: was he now acting not only as a decoy but also as a watch guard protecting his family?

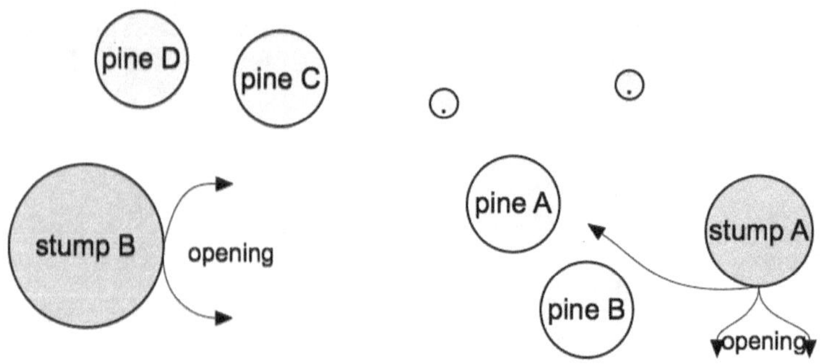

Figure 18 The area map

As shown in [Fig 18], two big pines trees, pine A and pine B, stood between stump A and stump B. In one of these two pine trees, I remembered a former hole created by a pileated woodpecker's nest in 2019.

Danny's behavior became even more complex. Instead of his usual perch, Danny began roosting high up in the pines C and D [Fig 18, 19] for the next four days and he revisited stump A for one day only. Had he perhaps not yet decided the optimal place from which to guard his family?

Figure 19 Danny hiding up high in a pine tree, looking at the nest, 4/16/2020

2.3 THE SECRET NEST

The nest hole built by pileated woodpeckers in 2019 [Fig 21] was big. Pileated woodpeckers are two and half times[4] larger than screech owls. For every nesting season, they can have two to three kids. [Fig 20] is an example of a pileated woodpecker nest I took in 2019 from another location.

Figure 20 A pileated woodpecker nest at another location, 2019

I revisited the hole [Fig 21] on April 19th and 20th. To my surprise, I saw nothing inside the hole, nor did I see any feathers or owl pellets near the hole. I was very disappointed but I decided to work harder and not give up.

---

4 Pileated Woodpecker size: 40-49cm (45cm in average). ESO size: 16-25 (20cm in average). Ref All about Birds Cornell.

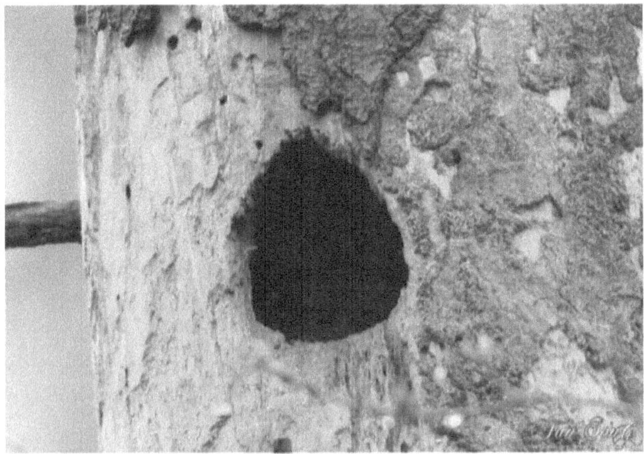

Figure 21 The disappointingly empty nest hole, 4/19/2020

In 2016 and 2018, I had seen the nests of two other screech owls. Those nest holes were just barely big enough for the screech owls to enter and exit [Fig 22]. I realized that a hole as big as the one in [Fig 21] would be a dangerous nesting place since their predators such as squirrels and raccoons could easily enter.

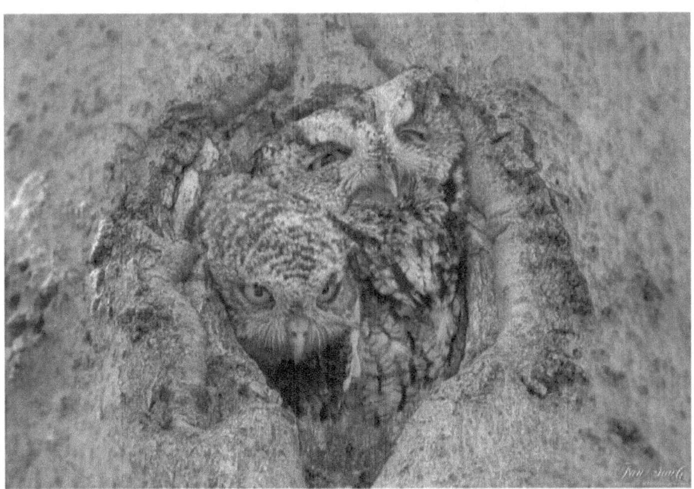

Figure 22 Mom and owlet squeezed in their tiny nest hole. Angrignon Park, Montreal 2018

I decided to stay late in the evening of April 21st. This time my patience paid off. I photographed Jane bringing food into their secret nest! Eureka! I finally found their nest [Fig 23]!

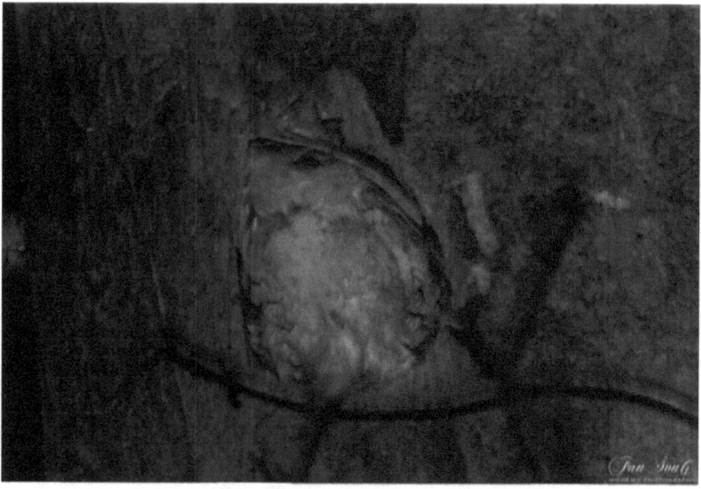

Figure 23 My eureka moment, Jane bringing food into the nest. 4/21/2018

3 NESTING

After two months of intricate speculations and ensuing investigations, it was very rewarding to have finally found the owls' nest [Fig 22]. I couldn't wait to see the owlets!

3.1 BRAVE DANNY

After days of indecision, Danny finally opted to perch at stump B [Fig 24] to perform his sentry duties.

Figure 24 Danny putting himself on public display, 4/19/2020

Every day he would perch there bravely as a decoy to distract people from discovering the screech owl babies [Fig 24, 25]. Since I knew his trick, I always made sure to salute him for his loyalty and dedication to his family.

Figure 25 Danny acting as a decoy, while keeping watch over his family, 4/20/2020

3.2 STEALTHY JANE

I was extremely anxious to see the owlets, but since Jane was so protective of her progeny, I was never able to see them appear up in the nest. I checked the nest daily and finally began to see Jane emerging from the hole [Fig 26]. Her comings and goings out of the nest meant the owlets were growing at a significant rate. She would need to start hunting more frequently to feed her owlets.

Figure 26 Stealthy Jane popping her head out the nest, 4/24/2020

Jane had a daily head start of about 10 to 15 minutes over Danny's schedule. She would come out of the nest and perch on her favorite branch for her preening and wing stretching exercises. While Danny was still bombarded by birders and photographers [Figure 28, 29], she already had started her pre-sunset hunting process. [Fig 27].

Figure 27 Jane hunting beside the pond before the sunset, 4/24/2020

3.3 FANS

The interactions between humans and the screech owls were also of particular interest to me. Since 2015, the screech owls would maintain a casual relationship with humans. The birders and photographers respected the screech owls and gave them privacy and the screech owls would maintain their routine, unbothered. Mind you, at the time, not many people knew about the presence of this family.

Since the nest was in plain sight right behind him, Danny's decoy strategy was successful as it fooled many onlookers. If anyone's camera skipped focus to deviate from Danny, it would immediately point to the spot where Jane was perching and nesting [Fig 28].

Figure 28 Fans taking pictures of Danny while neglecting Jane, 5/8/2020

To illustrate this point, I combined two sharp pictures of both parents into a single image to show the careful show the owls put on [Fig 29].

Figure 29 Danny and Jane in line of sight from each other, 5/8/2020

3.4 THE OWLETS AND SENTRY JANE

Research shows that owlets start to appear on the edge of their hole one week before they fledge. I counted the days to make sure I wouldn't miss this exciting event.

In the early morning of May 4th, I was ecstatic to see three fluffy heads pop up from inside the nest! [Fig 30, 31]

Figure 30 Two owlets perching on the edge of the nest. 5/4/2020

Figure 31 Three owlets popping their head out of the nest, 5/6/2020

The owlets were getting larger by the day. On May 5th, Jane was outside the nest roosting at stump A and acting as a sentry. [Fig 32, 4, 6, 16]. Danny was still watching at stump B, so their eyes would never leave the nest. This action was a huge indication that the owlets were so big that the parents had to move out. This also meant that the owlets were independent enough to be home alone.

Figure 32 Jane, the sentry, intently watching the nest from *stump A*, 5/5/2020

3.5 THE NEST SECRET IS NO MORE

"Two owls found! Two owls found!" The news spread like wildfire. Soon, waves of people flooded the forest, excited to see the family.

Rumors of the couple' nesting were also brewing. Birders and photographers came and inspected every potential nesting site.

Figure 33 Three cute owlets peeking from the nest, 5/9/2020

On May 8th, the public finally discovered the nest! Enjoy the pictures of three compact owlets huddled together in their nest! [Fig 33, 34]

Figure 34 Three cute owlets peeking from the nest. 5/11/2020

3.6 LAST DAY IN THE NEST

On May 13th, many people gathered in front of the nest, eagerly waiting to see the owlets emerge from it. Faced with a lot of cameras, the babies were extremely active after the sunset. One older owlet made its way out and stood on the very edge of the hole, crazily bobbing its head in an attempt to judge its nearby surroundings.

At 8:20p.m., almost in the dark [Fig 35], the brave owlet made its historical first jump! It immediately got stuck on some branches, but extraordinarily, the baby screech owl managed to set himself straight and fly to another pine tree. It then fell on the ground, hopping about like crazy on a twig of a dead tree, finally flying away into the dark woods [Fig 36]. It was really heartwarming to see the baby screech owl's small journey.

Figure 35 One visually annoyed owlet squished by another fledging owlet, 8:19p.m., 5/13/2020

Figure 36 One owlet fledging at 8:20p.m., 5/13/2020

4 THE OUTSIDE WORLD

This chapter explores the development of the owlets in their first 6 weeks of life in the outside world. It was touching to watch them grow and learn essential skills. However, as beautiful as their experience in the outside world was, it was also filled with dangers.

4.1 FIRST ADVENTURES

From May 13th to 15th, I witnessed the five owlets fledging one after the other. Watching the five "fluffy balls" hop around the forest gave me great joy. They would stumble from branch to branch, making clumsy attempts to fly [Fig 37-42].

Figure 37 Owlet #1 stuck in a V-shaped trunk junction (suspected male), 5/14/2020

Figure 38 Owlet #2 napping cozily in the shade (suspected male), 5/14/2020

Figure 39 Owlet #3 resting ungracefully (suspected male), 5/14/2020

Figure 40 Owlet #4 climbing up a tree trunk (suspected female), 5/14/2020

Figure 41 Owlet #5 posing on a small shrub close to the ground (suspected female - Anna), 5/15/2020

However, there was still one fledgling missing during my search that day.

Figure 42 Owlet #6 is nowhere to be seen, 5/15/2020

Judging from the size of the five owlets [Fig 37-41], the first three owlets to fledge were similar in size; the fourth and fifth owlets that ventured one or two days later were much larger. Christian [Ref 6] pointed out that generally, female screech owls take a longer time to develop in the nest and are warier of leaving. Out of the five owlets, two of them were suspected of being female.

It was amazing to see their flight rapidly improving after fledging. On the night of May 16th, all six owlets roosted on a pine tree nearly 10 meters high [Fig 43, 44, 45].

Figure 43 Five owlets snuggling together with the sixth one above them, 5/16/2020

Figure 44 Three owlets bathing in the golden sunset, 5/16/2020

4.2 ONE OWLET MISSING

After the sunset on May 16th, one owlet fell off a pine tree. At the time, Jane was leading the owlets into the maple woods and left the fallen screech owlet unattended. It must have died either from the fall or from predators. From then on, I only saw five owlets [Fig 45]. I felt remorseful for the unfortunate death of the sixth owlet. Nature is beautiful but also cruel and dangerous.

Figure 45 Five surviving owlets, 5/17/2020

4.3 THE NOMADS

After venturing from the nest, there was no fixed roosting place for the screech owl family. Usually, Danny would watch the owlets from a short distance away. Jane stayed very close to the owlets, protecting them. Each day, the final roosting site would be determined by Jane and their hunting location of the time. The final rooting site could be in dead tree trunks or in living maple or pine trees [Fig 46-51].

Figure 46 Five owlets nestling in a maple tree, 5/20/2020

Figure 47 The owlets huddling in another maple tree. 5/22/2020

Figure 48 The owlets cuddling in a very tall maple tree, 5/24/2020

Figure 49 Four owlets at top of a dead tree stump, 5/24/2020

Figure 50 Five owlets at top of another dead tree stump 5/31/2020

Figure 51 Jane and the owlets erecting their tufts in the woods, 6/5/2020

From May 14th to May 16th, in the first three days of their fledging process, the owlets spent most of their time adapting to the spring environment. Because of the mild winter, the screech family nesting behavior occurred two weeks earlier than normal. This made short distance flying easier for the owlets since there were not many tree leaves to complicate in-flight navigation.

The screech owl family lived a nomadic lifestyle during the first fledging week of the owlets. Each day, they would cover approximately a 500-meter radius. This was a lot of exercise for me! I kept all of their routes in my digital map so that I could continuously track them.

4.4 APPETITE

Raising five owlets was a huge and demanding task for Danny and Jane. However, due to the mild winter of 2020, there was an abundance of prey for the owls to hunt. For example, on May 21st, I saw Danny and Jane feed the owlets about 15 times in 15 minutes! That meant that every two minutes, a screech owl parent had to catch prey for one owlet.

Their prey consisted of a huge variety: moths, dragonflies, earth worms, ants, small fishes, frogs, baby squirrels and a wide range of songbirds [Fig 52-57].

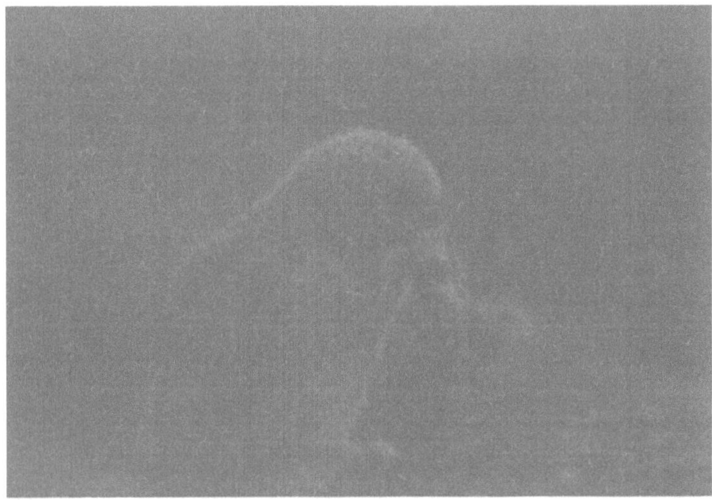

Figure 52 An owlet eating a female scarlet tanager (extracted from video), 5/23/2020

Figure 53 Jane catching a dragonfly, 6/2/2020

Figure 54 Jane feeding a moth to an owlet, 5/31/2020

Figure 55 Jane watching an owlet gulping down a dragonfly, 6/3/2020

Figure 56 An owlet eating a poor frog (extracted from video), 5/25/2020

Figure 57 An owlet eating a beetle (extracted from video), 6/9/2020

4.5 TWO WEEKS AFTER

The first three owlets fledged during the evening of May 13th and the morning of May 14th. Although the next owlets fledged on the 15th and the last one on the 16th, I use the date of May 14th as the average day of the owlets leaving the nest to explore the outside world. Thus, by May 27th, it had already been two weeks since they had left the nest [Fig 58].

During these two weeks, all five owlets had dramatically improved their flying skills. They could easily fly inside the dense foliage and dodge any small branch and twig. Keeping pace with their accomplished parents seemed to be a kind of racing game between the owlets. Whoever flew the best had the best chance to be fed first.

Figure 58 Owlet party, 5/27/2020

At this time, the owlets had almost grown to the size of their parents. Due to their down feathers, some appeared even bigger than their parents. [Fig 59-61].

Figure 59 Jane and an owlet, 5/29/2020

Figure 60 Jane and the smallest owlet (Sunny), 5/31/2020

Figure 61 The largest owlet and the smallest owlet (Anna and Sunny), 5/29/2020

I was waiting for a moment where all the screech owl family members would group together for a family picture. On June 1st, International Children's day, all the owlet 'children' were coincidently hanging out together with their mother. Twelve eyes were on me the entire time as I was taking the photo [Fig 62].

Figure 62 A special family portrait on International Children's Day (Jane and the five owlets), 6/1/2020

4.6 THREE WEEKS AFTER

June 4th marked the third week since the owlets had left the nest.

The five owlets were divided into two groups; a group of three and a group of two. The smallest owlet bonded with the largest one (suspected female) [Fig 63, 65]. The other three owlets formed the second group [Fig 64].

Figure 63 The largest owlet (Anna) preening the smallest owlet (Sunny), 6/2/2020

Figure 64 The naughty gang of three with Christine in the middle, 6/5/2020

From observing other owls such as great horned owls and barred owls, I knew there would often be one female in each group.

Figure 65 The duo (Anna and Sunny). 6/5/2020

Owlets start to hunt by themselves during this period. Anna, the largest owlet had started her hunting debut one week earlier [Figure 66]. Easy food such as ants, earth worms, and frogs were their favorite prey [Fig 66-69].

Figure 66 Anna catching a worm on the ground, 5/27/2020

Figure 67 An owlet raiding a bird's nest. 5/28/2020

Figure 68 An owlet catching a black ant. 5/31/2020

Figure 69 An owlet staring at a frog in the pond, failing to catch it. 6/4/2020

Food sharing was very common within the owlet family members. A couple of times I saw the largest owlet (Anna) sharing a meal with the youngest one Sunny [Fig 70].

Figure 70 Anna sharing a frog with Sunny - extracted from video. 6/6/2020

The owlets employed teamwork to catch more complicated prey. On June 9th, it took a team of two owlets to attack a red squirrel's nest.

One owlet stood guard outside, while the other one dived down into the dark hole. Earlier, the owlets had scared the squirrel mother away. The diving owlet came out with a baby squirrel still in its beak. Unfortunately, the owlet that dived into the hole didn't share the prey with his sibling. I could see that the one standing guard was very disappointed [Fig 71, 72].

Figure 71 The team attacking the red squirrel's nest. 6/9/2020

Figure 72 An owlet with a baby squirrel in its beak (extracted from video). 6/9/2020

4.7 ONE MONTH AFTER

June 13th marked one month since the owlets had left their nest.

4.7.1 PORTRAITS

[Fig 73-76] shows one owlet's back feathers. From this angle, its feathers really resemble an adult screech owl's ones.

Figure 73 A side portrait of an owlet, 6/11/2020

Figure 74 An owlet looking backwards 6/18/2020

Figure 75 A three-quarter portrait of three owlets, 6/19/2020

Figure 76 A front-facing portrait of Jane, looking at the camera (included in comparison with the owlets), 6/19/2020

The owlets' flying ability had become exceptionally precise and skilled. They no longer had to carefully maneuver their way around obstacles in the forest. Instead, they could now simply tuck in their wings and weave their way through. They were so fast that I had to watch them closely, otherwise they would be gone in the blink of an eye. They had also become very adept at hovering. Sometimes I saw them catching prey in mid-air.

4.7.2 NEST RAIDING

Around mid-May, other birds such as robins and starlings start to nest. Birds attempting to nest in the same forest as these owlets would soon realize their grave mistake.

Figure 77 Four owlets preparing to raid an unsuspecting bird's nest.
6/13/2020

As the owlets grew, they became more adventurous and developed a new hobby: raiding nests. The scheming owlets would gather on a branch close to the targeted nest. The leader of the gang would stealthily approach the nest, honing in on their prey. Obediently, the other owlets would follow one-by-one and perch patiently waiting for the opportune moment. The leader would calculate the distance from the nest by bobbing his head. In complete silence, the leader would suddenly swoop down on the nest and the rest of the owlets would follow suit. Feathers, leaves and twigs would then scatter the air while the birds being attacked were letting out piercing screams. [Fig 77, 78].

Figure 78 The leader of the raiding gang, 6/13/2020

4.7.3 CAMOUFLAGE

As a defensive technique, when alarmed by approaching danger, screech owls will erect their tufts, compress their feathers, and elongate themselves so they appear more like a broken branch [Fig 79]. They may even sway back and forth to imitate the natural movements of a branch.

Figure 79 Two owlets adopting a vertically elongated body shape to camouflage themselves as a tree trunk, 6/23/2020

4.8 SIX WEEKS AFTER

Around six weeks after leaving the nest, the adult feather plumage pattern was starting to show on one of the oldest owlets' breast. The adult barb pattern was more visible among its baby feather pattern of wavy lines. [Fig 80].

Figure 80 An owlet with nascent adult plumage on its breast, 6/26/2020

Figure 81 Fringed edges of an owlet's flight feathers, 6/25/2020

[Fig 81] shows the tiny serrations on the leading edges of an owlet's flight feathers. The fringed edges muffled the sound of owls' wings so that prey would not hear them coming. Their stealth and speed made them deadly to their prey.

The summer of 2020 was extremely hot. One might wonder how the owlets can survive such temperatures with so many feathers covering their bodies.

Figure 82 An owlet responding to high temperatures, 6/22/2020

As shown in [Fig 82], a screech owlet has its eyes half open, wings sluggishly extended, and beak panting.

5 GROWING INTO INDEPENDENCE

Many questions came to mind as the five owlets grew daily.

When will they leave their parents?

Will their parents chase them away? Or will the owlets depart on their own?

What will happen when the owlets leave? Will they establish their own territory and where?

Will they come back to visit their parents? Will they still recognize their parents?

5.1 MOLTING

On June 26th, I had the opportunity to watch Jane and an owlet stretching their wings and their bodies [Fig 83]. This gave me a good side by side view of their size and plumage. The biggest difference was in their plumage. Jane had head, face and collar stripes, while her breast was layered with "barb" shaped patterns and the owlet only had a sort of horizontal wave patterns.

Figure 83 The plumage difference between Jane (right) and an owlet, 6/26/2020

As noted in [sec 4.8], the owlets started molting around week 6 [Fig 80]. July 3rd was the first time I was able to distinguish between the owlets due to their noticeably different molting patterns [Fig 84]. I named them: Anna, Alex, Christine, Charles and Sunny. Before this point, it was impossible to tell them apart, let alone name them.

Figure 84a Anna, Alex and Christine

Figure 84b Charles and Sunny, 07/03/2020

[Fig 84] showed that Anna had molted about 20% of her breast feathers, while Sunny still showed no signs of molting. It also showed their molting patterns progressed downwards from the neck to the feet.

5.2 GROUPING AND BONDING

I had concluded there were at least two females among the five owlets by their distinct behaviors [Sec 4.1]. In last chapter, I referred the group of the largest owlet and the smallest one as the "duo", and the other owlets as the "gang of three".

After I had managed to tell each owlet apart by their molting pattern, the close relationship and affection between Alex, Christine and Charles seemed to indicate that they were the "gang of three" in [Sec 4.6]; while Anna, the last one to fledge [Fig 41] and Sunny were the "duo". The two groups showed great solidarity, hunting together and preening together [Fig 85, 86]. This also proved that each group had one female.

This begs the question: would these owlets eventually become partners and mate during a future nesting season?

Figure 85 Sunny and Anna preening each other, 7/5/2020

Figure 86 Charles and Christine "kissing" each other, 7/5/2020

I concluded that Sunny was male since he would always stay close to either Jane, the mother, or Anna. [Fig 87].

It is difficult and unreliable at best to determine the sex of a screech owl by size alone. This is where behaviour becomes more telling. Anna was the last one to leave the nest and survive. We will never know what gender the sixth was, but I suspect a female. Based on Christian's observation on peregrine falcons, female chicks are often the last to leave the nest. I believe his theory applies here as well [Ref 6].

I observed that the owlets were copying their parents' preening behaviors. Their grooming behaviours and preening positions within each group helped me identify the sex of each owlet [Fig 85, 86, 87]. For example, the male preens the female more in this family. The female owlet in the duo was named Anna and the one in the gang of three Christine.

The owlets would preen each other for five to ten minutes before setting out for the nightly hunt and on their return to roost for the day. In [Fig 85] the male owlet Sunny is gently holding the foot of the female owlet Anna and carefully "combing" her tuft feathers. During this time, Anna is seemingly enjoying the experience.

Figure 87 Sunny preening Jane, 7/15/2020

Watching the owlets' mutual preening reminded me of the courtship rituals between Jane and Danny in April [Fig 12, 13, 14]. This important pair-bonding ritual is not just associated with courtship, but can occur in siblings too!

I believe that owlets forming groups among themselves help them develop and change into adulthood faster as they learn from each other.

Again, is it too far-fetched to project that these owlets could eventually form couples?

5.3 PREDATORS AND THREATS

There were a number of forest predators in the woods the owlets had to be alert to avoid.

Figure 88 A feral cat, 7/13/2020

[Fig 88] This feral cat prowled around and watched the owlets from time to time. The owlets had a few close encounters with this cat. When that happened, it was an intense and humorous scene as both parties would have their ears and tufts perked up, with their eyes open wide and staring at each other.

Figure 89 A Cooper's hawk, 7/20/2020

[Fig 89] The Cooper's hawk was another big threat as it lived in the same area. The Cooper's hawk usually hunted in a higher part of the canopy than where the owlets stayed. However, thanks to its silent flying skills and high manoeuvrability through the woods, it could swoop down silently to capture its prey, posing a serious danger to the owlets.

Figure 90 The Intruder – the Great horned owl, 7/2/2020

[Fig 90] The great horned owl was an occasional intruder in the area. His appearance was no doubt a huge threat to the screech owl family. I only saw him once so far but there is no doubt that he will visit the screech owls' territory more frequently in the coming fall.

Figure 91 Raccoons, 7/18/2020

[Fig 91] There were at least three or four raccoon families nearby this year. One family had five little ones. Raccoons are a notorious threat to all kinds of birds, especially at night.

5.4 OWLET DISPERSAL

On July 8th, about two months after fledging, Christine and Charles left home, and I never saw them again.

Christine and Charles' departure meant that Alex was on his own. However, interestingly, Anna and Alex soon formed a new bond - a result of natural selection to me. And this proved that Alex was a male. In the following days, on July 13th, Anna and Alex left the territory as well.

On July 20th, Sunny, the last owlet, left too.

All the questions raised at the beginning of the chapter were gradually answered. The five growing owlets and their parents consumed a lot of food during this two-month period. At first, their food was mostly insects and other small prey. But, as the owlets grew older, their main food sources were chipmunks, frogs and birds. The owlets needed to look for places with a more abundant food source and easy-to-catch prey since there was not much left in their home territory.

The owlets' departure decisions were shaped by two factors: their flying and hunting skills, and separation from their parents. The teamwork of the groups greatly accelerated their growth into independence. Once they became confident in flying and hunting, it would be a natural thing for them to leave the native territory for a new one.

Secondly, Jane and Danny had been distancing themselves from the owlets lately. They would not roost in the vicinity of where the owlets were resting. When the owlets could not find their parents, they would choose a secret place to hide and roost during the day. After a few days of separation from their parents, they became more independent and were ready to find territories of their own.

"All good things must come to an end". From the very beginning of my journey with this owl family, I had always known that the owlets would leave some day. I was thrilled that the five owlets were independent enough to venture out of their own but I felt sombre at their departures and concerned that the new and unfamiliar territories could put them in unforeseen dangers.

In the past 6 months, I watched Danny and Jane raising the owlets and teaching them life skills. I witnessed the five owlets developing from helpless nestlings to curious fledglings taking their first tentative flights to confident juveniles launching into independence. After spending so much time with them, I established a special bond with each member of the family. Just as I can easily identify each of them, I have no doubt that they learned to recognize my face and allowed me to approach them and get much closer than they would have let others. They had provided my family with great joy and emotional sustenance. They were part of my family.

My family felt sad at the loss of "our owlet family members". It was good that they stayed out of sight and carried on their separate lives. The owlets had yet to master news skills and knowledge to survive in their new territories. We wish they will make it through their lives successfully. We may meet them again someday!

5.5 JANE'S RETURN AND MOLT

Nearly a week after the owlets had dispersed, Jane returned to tree stump A. The stump was an old but familiar place for her. After two months of hard work and nurturing, it was time for her to relax.

Figure 92 Jane's return to tree stump A, 7/21/2020

Jane's return marked the end of my 6-month project with the family. It was a long and sweet journey but it also left many questions:

Jane started to molt a few days after her return. On Aug 11th, she was totally bald on head and face. Do screech owls molt when the fall comes or do they molt after each nesting?

Where is Danny? I have a feeling that he is with some of the owlets and still watching them. I will wait for the fall/winter season to find out the answer.

How far are the owlet's new territories away from their native site? Will they return to their native habitat before the winter comes or the following spring?

Maybe you'll find out all the answers in my next screech owl book!

6 PHOTO GALLERY 2020

This section includes my most memorable screech owl pictures. Most pictures were taken during the breeding season between Feb 2020 and July 2020 and the majority of the pictures are about the life of the five owlets during their first two months of adventure in the outside world.

These pictures provide an intimate access to the screech owl in ways never seen before. Enjoy!

Figure 93 Danny's camouflage, 2018

Figure 94 Jane's camouflage in tree *stump C* [2], Feb, 2020

Figure 95 Danny in the light of the golden sunset, 2018

Figure 96 Jane's camouflage, Feb 2020

Figure 97 Eastern screech owl (red morph), Toronto, 2017

Figure 98 Two curious screech owlets in the nest

Figure 99 Two shy owlets in the nest

Figure 100 A screech owlet (a suspected male)

Figure 101 One owlet leaning on another one

Figure 102 Owlet #5 (a suspected female Anna)

Figure 103 Danny in the light of the golden sunrise

Figure 104 Jane's portrait

Figure 105 The two biggest owlets (suspected: Anna & Christine)

Figure 106 An owlet on the prowl

Figure 107 Anna hunting at ground level

Figure 108 An inquisitive owlet

Figure 109 Four big, round eyes

Figure 110 An owlet on the road

Figure 111 Can you tell which is Jane?

Figure 112 The whispering duo

Figure 113 Three alerting owlets

Figure 114 The winking Owlet

Figure 115 Jane squinting her eyes

Figure 116 Regal Danny

Figure 117 Four pensive owlets

Figure 118 Three mischievous owlets about to raid a nest

Figure 119 Three owlets with innocent looks

Figure 120 The duo on the hunt

Figure 121 Two playing owlets

Figure 122 What a surprise find, a worm on the ground

Figure 123 The gang of three

Figure 124 A lovely duo in the woods

Figure 125 The duo on alert

Figure 126 Sneaky Anna

Figure 127 Alex

Figure 128 Christine

Figure 129 Charles

Figure 130 Last sight of Sunny. Notice his latest molt pattern

IMPORTANT DATES (2020)

Feb 5th: A screech owl was first seen on stump C

Feb 11th: Two screech owls were reported

Mar 11th: Danny started to roost on stump A

Apr 2nd: My first sighting of Jane

Apr 13th: Danny first showed up on stump B

Apr 19th: Danny settled down on stump B

Apr 19th: First sighting of the courtship

Apr 21st: First picture of Jane feeding the owlets in the nest

Apr 24th: First sighting of Jane roosting in the nest

May 4th: First sighting of the three owlets in the nest

May 5th: Jane perched on stump A as droves of people arrived

May 8th: The nest was found by the public

May 13-15th: Six owlets left the nest

May 16th: One owlet missing after sunset

May 27th: Two weeks after the owlets left the nest

June 4th: Three weeks after the owlets left the nest

June 6th: The owlets started hunting in groups

June 11th: Four weeks after the owlets left the nest

June 13th: One month after the owlets left the nest

July 3th: First differentiation of the five owlets by their molting patterns

July 8th: Third and fourth owlets (Christine and Charles) left the site

July 13th: First and second owlets (Anna and Alex) left the site

July 13th: Two months after the owlets left the nest

July 20th: The fifth owlet (Sunny) left the site

July 21st: Jane's return to tree stump A

August 11st: Jane started molt in stump A

REFERENCES

[1] Eastern screech owl (male) preening, yawning and stretching before sunset: https://youtu.be/DK5qmWQ3GR8

[2] Eastern screech owl (female) roosting on a tree stump: https://youtu.be/lGUA6tlDThw

[3] The complete guide to the barred owl nesting in the beaver trail of Wild Bird Care Center from 2017 to 2020: https://fsong00.wordpress.com/2020/05/26/barred-owl-nest-at-wild-bird-care-center-ottawa-the-complete-guide-from-2017-2020/

[4] Eastern screech owl life history – The Cornell Lab, All About Birds https://www.allaboutbirds.org/guide/Eastern_Screech-Owl/lifehistory

[5] Screech-owl breeding behavior: https://www.barnowlbox.com/screech-owl-breeding-behavior/

[6] Christian Fritschi's photography site: https://christianfritschi.com/

[7] Christian Fritschi's bird photography on Flickr: https://www.flickr.com/photos/cfphotographs/albums

[8] Eastern screech-owl and downy woodpecker: https://youtu.be/1UZMx0i9UAE

[9] Eastern screech-owl at Mud Lake: https://youtu.be/0i-0TrzuQLw

[10] Eastern screech-owl nest at Agrignon park 2018: https://youtu.be/2c9Txd-XSCM

[11] Fan Song Photography Youtube Channel: https://www.youtube.com/fsong00

[12] eBird report www.ebird.org

[13] Eastern Screech-Owl Wiki: https://en.wikipedia.org/wiki/Eastern_screech_owl

[14] Bird watching eastern screech-owl: https://www.birdwatchingblog.us/breeding-season-2/eastern-screech-owl.html

[15] PSU eastern screech-owl: https://www.psu.edu/dept/nkbiology/naturetrail/speciespages/screechowl.html

[16] Owl pages: https://www.owlpages.com/owls/species.php?s=850

[17] 8 owls you might hear at night: https://www.treehugger.com/owls-you-might-hear-night-4868764

[18] Anna and red-morphed screech at stump E: https://youtu.be/M9erlnm1-qk

AUTHOR

Fan Song (fsong00@gmail.com) is a network engineer working in the Ottawa, Canada high-tech sector, a passionate birder and wildlife photographer since 2001. Owls are Fan's favorite subject. He has done extensive and meticulous research on native owls such as the great horned owl (GHO), barred owl (BO), and eastern screech owl (ESO). His main observation objects from 2010 to 2020 were mainly large species GHO and BO. After 2020, Fan began to conduct more research and observations on small ESOs. ESOs have wonderful lives and people ignore them because they are small and hard to be spot during the day. After careful research, Fan published the trilogy for ESOs: The secret life of the eastern screech owl, Prequel, and Sequel.

He won the first prize of 2020 Nature Canada and second prize of Uqrop 2018 photo contest. More of his work can be seen online in the following venues:

www.youtube.com/cuteowls4u

www.instagram.com/fsong00

www.tiktok.com/@thecuteowls

www.flickr.com/photos/fsong_travel

As a Computer Science and Electrical Engineer, building drones and all kinds of Computer Numerical Control (CNC) machines are also a part of Fan's hobbies.

https://www.youtube.com/fsong00/

Blog at Wordpress:

https://fsong00.wordpress.com/

SPECIAL CONTRIBUTION

Christian Fritschi (email: chr.fritschi@gmail.com)

Christian Fritschi is a retired eclectic photographer who has been devoting much of the past few years to bird observation and photography. He is also a volunteer at the Raptor's Rehabilitation Center (Chouette à Voir) and the Raptor's Clinic in the Province of Québec (UQROP). He has participated in several rescue and release missions since 2015.

Additionally, in the Winter, he takes part in Snowy owl relocation endeavors. Snowy owls have the bad habit of stopping over at the Montreal International Airport for a break on their migratory path. The open fields surrounding the runways offer plenty of hunting opportunities for the snowies but at the same time constitute a real danger to the birds and the planes' safety.

https://www.uqrop.qc.ca/en/

https://www.falconenvironmental.com/fr/

TRILOGY

[BOOK I]: The Secret Life Of The Eastern Screech Owl (Amazon English black and white ISBN 979-8677671555, English color ISBN 979-8677572531, French ISBN 979-8550564882, German ISBN 979-8586598813)

[BOOK II]: The Prequel Secret Life Of The Eastern Screech Owl (Amazon English ISBN 979-8836442248)

[BOOK III]: The Sequel Secret Life Of The Eastern Screech Owl (Amazon English ISBN 979-8836436919)